This book is a gift of love from:

_____

To:

I0160743

_____

Dedicated to my mother Odette,
my father Augustin,
my sister Endji,
and my brothers Ford and Eden.

Thank you for being poetry in my life,
even when my life refused to rhyme.

Rhyme Heals All Wounds.

Life and Love,
Journeyed Through Poetry.

Written by: Lenz Dalusma
Illustrated by: Bianca J. Russell

Rhyme Heals All Wounds.

ISBN: 978-0-692-05197-9

Contact:

LenzDalusmaPoetry@gmail.com

Instagram/Twitter: @RhymeAndShine
Facebook.com/RhymeAndShineMinistry
RhymeAndShine.org

Dear Reader,

I know love and life are complicated. Therefore, I've taken the liberty of gathering every emotion you've ever felt, every sadness, every joy, every confusion, and I've carefully crafted them in poetic form just for you.

So, whatever phase you are in when it comes to love and life, I guarantee that you will find a few poems in here that will speak to your soul.

This book is the result of a decade of writing and the works included were diligently selected.

Enjoy!!!

Rhyme Heals All Wounds...

I. <u>**FRIENDSHIPS & FROWNS**</u>

Friendship is one of life's greatest gift. It brings comfort, reliability, inside jokes, and, occasionally, a lifetime bond.

*But, other times, **friendship is the worst!***

I'm talking about those times when friendship unexpectedly abracadabras its way into your life. And then, once you've been magnet'd into its trap, it pulls off its mask and bam...Friendship becomes love. You've been bamboozled!

How do you escape this? Do you ignore those feelings? Do you dare bring up that 4-letter L-word to your "friend"? What if the feeling's not mutual?

*This chapter explores the fear, the uncertainty, and the pain of only being a friend, when you want to be more. That's when it feels as if **friendship is the absolute worst!***

Best Friend

You are a blessing
and the best friend
I've ever had.
You are the good that outweighs all of my bad.

We've shared a chapter of laughter
and had quite an adventure.
I love you more than I ever
thought that I'd venture.

So here I am on my knees
asking you please
"Will you make me a stranger?"

Because while sailing on this friend-ship,
I have fallen overboard
into a sea of love that I cannot overcome.

But you say "friends" is all we are meant to be.
And that's an entity
you value with sanctity.

When you asked if I'd be fine,
I crossed my heart and hoped to lie.

And I tried to go on as usual.
As if life is still beautiful.

But in your presence, I suffer
knowing you'll never be my lover.

Your smile smites me. Your beauty is murder.
Your passion is a poison
I can't take any further.

I've been doing my best
to try to keep my death away.
But you keep being yourself,
and it's taking my breath away.

I fell into your felony.
This friendship may become the end of me.
Your perfection has become my enemy.

So, I am sorry.
But you can no longer star in my story.
I cannot bear to stare
at the glare of your glory.

As my feelings deepen,
I cannot depend
on my ability to survive
as I'm being burned by the light of your shine.

I am cursed to feel the way I do.
But because I love you, I cannot like you.

So, pardon me,
but you can no longer be part of me.

You have become
my greatest danger.
So please, I beg you,
just make me a stranger.

Carpe DM

Emojis of smiley faces.
Heart-to-heart on how our day is.
Corny jokes that just a-maizes.
Profound talks of life's next phases.

Flirty text to test my limit,
I could do it every minute.

A.M. or P.M.,
I slide in her DM
and I carpe diem.

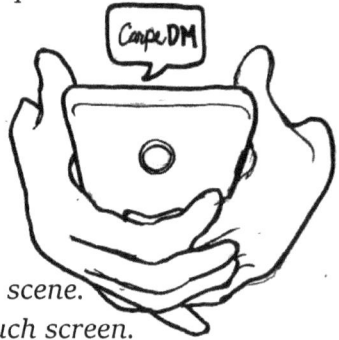

I turn her inbox into a love scene.
I'm so tough behind my touch screen.

But in her presence, I've tried
to say even more.
Yet my tongue gets tied
like an even score.

Because I don't want to say much,
before I say too much.

I'm not yet willing to be spilling
all I'm feeling and such.

I'm losing my fight
against fright.

I let my fears
cover my ears
so I don't hear
the words of wisdom's whisper

telling me
that she may be
much more than merely another sister.

I let my own lies
cover my brown eyes
so I don't recognize
what I've already known.
Yet my mind has a mind of its own.

And it speaks the words I've never said.
Sips of her lips run laps in my head.

Her eyes, they freeze me.
Her smile, it frees me.

I've fallen in feelings that I can't stop.
She draws me in like Photoshop.

Her charisma
carries my
heart on a race of many miles.

And a piece
of her peace
can soothe my soul for an eternal while.

I love her sense of humor.
I love her sense of human.
I love her sense of woman.

I grow mellow in
the glow of her melanin.

Her presence blesses.
She keeps me restless.
I don't need Gollum to know she's precious.

She pulls on my heart strings like tug-of-war.
I'm convinced she is...well, let me say no more.

Because I don't want to say much
before I say too much.

I'm not yet willing to be spilling
all I'm feeling and such.

When it comes to love lives
I know that soft guys
never make the cut, like dull knives.

So, I will never tell her.
But I hope she feels the signs like Helen Keller.

I won't wear my heart on my sleeves,
I'll return it to my hollow chest.
It will be my treasure chest

Never the less,
my feelings will never be less.
So, I guess...

I'll just keep turning her inbox into a love scene.
Because I'm so tough behind my touch screen.

Him

There she goes again
with that man
I like to call "Him".

Him is the apple of her eye
and the man of her dreams.
Her heart's better half
and the one that she needs.

But every now and again,
Him breaks her heart to sand.

That's when I come in
with the broom and the pan
to sweep up all that I can.

Then, with my surgical hands
get her heart to mend
and tend to her demands
just to end the tears of a friend.

But as her frown's erased
and replaced
with a smile on her face,

7

in comes Mr. Prince Charming
on his white horse
named "Baby, I'm sorry."

With that, he taketh his darling
and he rides off,
leaving sorrows back for me.

Her heart is a lock without a key,
it can never be opened.

The only men who can enter
are those who can render
her heart to be broken.

She's addicted to the heartbreak,
which I cannot provide.
But how much hurt can a heart take
until it cannot survive?

This princess is seeking for
one of those "Happy Ends.
But how often must she kiss the frog
before she knows it's not a Prince?

She's so occupied
with trying to find
her happy ending,

she fails to realize
that her "happy" is ending.

She cannot tell that her fairy tale
is becoming a fairly scary tale.

So, it will be of no surprise
when she returns with tear-filled eyes

with her heart crumbled to dust,
but I'll be there to sweep
although I know that it won't sweep
Weeping Beauty off her feet.

I'll be there to care and listen
as she complains that no man
is ever there to care or listen.

I'll treat her like a Queen,
because she deserves it.
Because she has earned it.

She will get the best from me,
because she is worth it.
She just hasn't learned it.

The tears on her cheeks screams her pain,
yet she hasn't heard it.

The story on this page, she cannot sustain,
yet she cannot turn it.

The bridge back to his arms drives her insane,
yet she cannot burn it.

So, I'll be the loving that she lacks
until "Baby, I'm sorry" comes trotting back.

Then there she'll go again
with that man
I like to call Him.

Halo

I was born a human,
but my parents had foreseen.
I'd grow up to be a Saint,
like the team in New Orleans.

So, from the womb
I was doomed
to live as an angel and
become a gentleman.

Ever since I was a little
baby in the cradle
my parents placed over my head a halo

which I have been able
to maintain stable
wherever I may go.

But already,
this halo has gotten so hard to carry.
For this light isn't light, it's pretty darn heavy.

Though I'm doing my best to keep it steady,
it is burning my scalp which is turning scary.

Oh, dear me in this head light.
I'm feeling like a deer in headlights.
But I'm trying to keep my head right
so I can keep my courtesy.
But courtesy really hurts, you see?

I'm not sure I can remain on this.
No good deed ever goes unpunished.
Planted seeds too often don't flourish.
Even Oz cannot give me courage.

I don't feel
I can fulfill
this quite lonely task

of always trying
to walk the line
like I'm Johnny Cash

as everyone else
makes for themselves
and go running past,

leaving my wandering mind
wondering "Why
must nice guys finish last?"

Well, I'm tired of knowing I'm meant to lose.
I'm tired of walking in "Nice Guy" shoes.

I'm tired of being covered
and colored
with "Nice Guy" blues.
And though I'm used to being tired,
I am tired of being used.

Much of me is demanded
but to be candid
all that's ever granted
is that I'll be taken for granted.

So, I think it's time to end it.

I mean it,
this minute

I am throwing in the towel
with my blood, sweat, and tears in it.
Why bother race when I know
I'm too gentleman to win it?

So, I am done
biting my tongue
or I'll soon talk with a lisp.
No more turning the other cheek,
my neck can no longer twist.

Being a gentleman had at once been pleasant,
but I've lost my interest, like a bad investment.

If someone wants to take my place,
be my guest, my plus one.
But the gentleman club, you have now lost one.

Oh, sweet victory.
No longer will I suffer from the misery
of chivalry.

Because ladies can't handle
the shine of a halo.

Open the door to their car
and it closes the door to their heart.

You call a lady beautiful
and you've given her the cue to go.

Because the most gorgeous girls
are the most self-conscious.
And the first-class ladies
are the last to know this,
I've noticed.

Those who make up the first tier
always shed the first tear,
but they'll still avoid the halo,
for that is their worst fear.

So, I've said my last hello
to this halo.

This little light of mine,
I'm going to let it die.

I'm going to snatch it
and scratch it.
And smash it. And slash it.
And bash it. And crash it.
And trash it.
And toss it in traffic.
It's tragic.

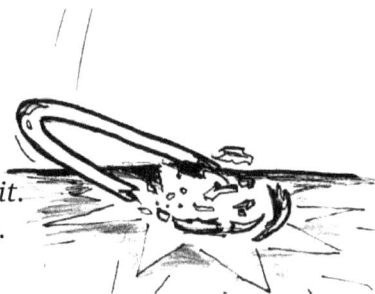

They told me chivalry was dead,
but I chose to be a skeptic.
I've spent my life trying to play God
hoping to resurrect it.

But now I know this
is hopeless.

Chivalry is dead.
It took a bullet to the head.
And women committed the murder.
She hoped nobody heard her.

But it's the truth.
Yes, the proof
is in the pudding,
so I'm putting
my foot down.

This is my resignation,
I may, one day, be back around.

It's my request
that, one day, a man's respects
won't always bring him regrets

because the ladies of the Earth
would have recognized their worth.

Maybe one day!

But until then,
my name is no longer penciled in
the stupid Book of Gentlemen.

Love for a Moment

Broken-hearted Beauty,
may I love you for a moment?
Your heart belongs to another. Yes, I know it.

Though he does not want it, you're sure he will.
And he'll someday come for your love, but still,

may I love you in the meanwhile?
I mean well.

Never you mind
that you'll never be mine.

After all, I am average
and your perfection is on overage.

But take advantage of my timing
and let me love you for the time being.

Let me love you,
as you get closer to closure.
Let me love you,
as you look over your cold shoulder.

I'm not asking for your returned love.
I'll give you my all. You just give me enough.

Let me love you.

Let me tend to your heart with tenderness.
When he returns,
you may wipe away my fingerprints.

Then deliver your heart to him. Signed, sealed.
Just return my heart
from the bottom of your high heels.

And I
promise
not to
let my
feelings
affect
the
way
that
I feel.

II.   *FEELINGS & FALSE-FLAGS*

So, you've found someone who is loving and kind and funny and...they're gone! Why does this always happen? You try to no longer catch feelings, but feelings still catch you.

This chapter took your teardrops and turned them into words. If you're brave enough to re-experience the heartbreak, go ahead and proceed through these next few poems.

Free

Her spirit is free.

*Not trapped in the prison cell
that their reasons sell.*

Her spirit is free.

*Not following the womanual
she's been told is the natural.*

Her spirit is free.

*She lives by her own accord.
Not for an award.
Nor to be adored.*

*Yet many men won't come aboard.
Her train of thought,
they find abhorrent.
They want her mindset aborted.*

*They find her too absurd
to absorb,
so they do not applaud
that her spirit is free.*

> *I guess free is too high of a price
> for a poor man to afford.*

Table For Two

From a meeting of the eye
to a greeting with a "Hi".

To "Beautiful name,
is it spelled with an "e" or an "i"?
To "Make sure it is saved
and hit me up anytime."

To "Table for two."
and "A dozen lilies for you."

To long walks with held hands.
and mental wedding bell plans
and "I can't wait to tell friends."

To "You look blue-tiful in that turquoise dress"
and "This was wonderful.
Let me escort you to your home address."

To "I guess this is good night."
and seeing sadness in your green eyes.
To "Will you be a gentleman
and carry me to my Queen Size"?

Which led to slow jams
and slow dance
and roaming through romance

and passing through passion
and acing those actions
that makes the sun hide its eyes
behind the horizon.

To us realizing tonight was perfect
and it would be best to always preserve it.

This is how I want to remember you
and have you remember me.
Any further interactions
may damage this beautiful memory.

So, let us end on a high
before heartache comes without a warning.
Let us love through the night
and I'll be forever gone by the morning.

Acrophobia (Fear of Heights)

Is my heart beating,
or is it taking a beating?

I don't like this feeling.
I fear what I'm seeing.

This lady lifts me so high, but I'm acrophobic.
I don't want to be up here, but I cannot control it.

So, I stand on this cliff so high above.
And if I don't watch my steps, I may fall...in love.

But she wants me to fall. I will never do so.
Love is a place where only the fools go.

So, I stand my ground as she looks up to me.
But before I knew it, I'm bounded by her beauty.

Then she pulls me with her smile.
I put up a fight.
I refuse to be pulled to a fall from this height.

Then she pulls me with her style,
but still I stayed strong.
I refuse to be pulled to a tumble this long.

But then, at this sight,
she gathers her might.

And she pulls me with her kiss.
Now I'm on the side of this cliff.

I hold on for dear life, as she pulls on my leg.
As thoughts race through my head,
my only choice is to beg.

So, I scream "Please, don't make me fall
from a distance so tall!

Won't you come up and grab a hold of my arm?"
But this lady has no mercy,
she pulls me with her charm.

Oh, my. She's ruthless,
Why did she do this?
I'm falling so quickly
and I'm feeling quite foolish.

Falling at the speed of light.
Oh, how I wish I could fly.

And darn you, gravity,
why aren't you grabbing me?
Why must you be so unkind?

I guess it is no lie, I am falling for her.
I must be a fool because I'm falling for her.

Falling with no parachute, my face to the skies.
Maybe if I close my eyes,
I can fight back my cries.

But then I realize...
This feeling is nice.

This rush
is so much.

This adrenaline
is fit for a gentleman.

Being up in the air,
and feeling the wind in my hair.

Knowing love's arm is there
to catch me with care.

Why was I so scared to take this leap of faith?
Not falling for her would have been the mistake.

I am glad love attacked.
I'm ready to be caught.
So catch me, my love, with all that I've got.

As I'm falling down, falling fast, falling back.
And then just like that, I went SPLAT!
And fell flat on my back.

What a fall.
I guess she's no longer there, after all.

Unlucky-In-Love

Let me tell you the story of
Ms. Unlucky-In-Love.

Ms. Unlucky-In-Love
was never lucky enough
when it comes to relationships.
But she wouldn't give up on this.

She had to find her soul mate
to help her smile like Colgate.

So, every day she prayed
"Lord, send me a man.
Amen!" And then,

she embarked on a quest
to find her other half.
Not knowing how long
the journey would last.

But finding Mr. Right
became quite
the torture.
The sharpest brother
was the first to cut her.

The smoothest guys
were the first to slide.
And those who were hip
were not by her side.

25

It was very alarming
that every Prince Charming
should have come with a warning.

She had many suitors,
but they didn't suit her.

She wanted a manly figure,
but got to figure
that on average
these men acted half her age.

Indeed,
their deeds
had the signature
of an immature.

And she grew tired of men
who swim
in the juveNile river.

She searched for a good omen,
but no men she roped in
could have tied the knot.
The arrow of Cupid must have missed its shot.

The best-groomed men
wouldn't make the best groom.
And some would jump a bridge
before they would jump the broom.

Now this miss
is tired of being dismissed.

All the hookup crashes
are giving her whiplash.

And all she asks is
for a man to marry
and to be merry
like Christmas.

There came a point in time
when she thought to herself
she had found Mister Right,
too bad that mister left.

Just like that, every man became an ex-man
like Wolverine.
Every picture-perfect partner
became cropped from the photo scene.

Now marriage
has become a mirage.

So, she cries: "This is becoming my worst fear.
My layers of prayers, did they fall on deaf ears?"

She keeps shooting for a mister
to make her a missus,
yet she always misses.

But, the truth is her mister missed her.
For God sent him long ago to assist her.

But he couldn't catch her attention.
Because her attention advanced in
too many directions.

Wasting days on these men she chases.
Looking for love in all the wrong faces.

She wonders if her endeavor will end, ever.
She's praying tomorrow will bring better.

But above all else, she should God her heart
and wait on the Lord.

But those words from the Pastor passed her.

So, she's still there in the fast lane
in search of a last name
and still bearing the past pain
of being Ms. Unlucky-In-Love.

Numbered

She dated a chef, but had a longer hunger.
She was courted by an accountant,
but those days were numbered.

She tested a lawyer who didn't pass her bar.
She flirted with a broker, he broke her heart.
She spoke to a shepherd, but he never herd her.
She dated a mortician, it felt like murder.

She tried a musician, but the fat lady sang.
She talked to a teacher, but the final bell rang.
She tried an examiner who failed her test.
She met a cop so boring, she fell under a rest.

She asked out a model who simply, oh, posed.
She opened up to a tailor,
but he kept his heart clothes.

There was a podiatrist
who got off on the wrong foot.
There came a baseball star
who then ran home soon.

She found a quarterback so fly,
sadly he never touched down.
Oh, how she searched for love,
but tears were all that she found.

Dear Love

Dear Love,

Hope told me you'd be coming soon.
But I've waited July through June

with the clock
tattooed to my eyes.
Yet, you've still not arrived.

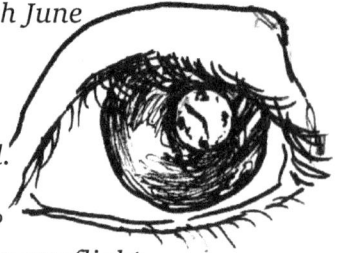

You are still coming, right?
Tell me you merely missed your flight.

Yes,
I bet
that's it.

Your alarm wasn't set
and you blindly overslept.
Am I correct?
Please tell me that I'm correct!

I can no longer bare this effect
of being so unpleasant.
I need to see your beauty,
if only for one second.

I need a kiss of bliss
to bless my face.
I'm in the midst of this
loneliness I can't erase.

So, Love, book another ticket to come visit.
I'll be waiting right here, I sure won't miss it.

On you, I depend.
Upon arrival, I'll cater to your heart's demand.

I cannot wait to see your sight!
You are still coming...right?

Hollow

Her loving is leaving.
Her eyes, they show me.

Her feelings have fallen.
I'll soon be lonely.

I've tried to swallow my sorrow,
but the hints haunt me slowly.

Even her hello sounds hollow,
it used to sound holy.

III. *FAILURES & FORGIVENESS*

The Bible tells us we are the light of the world. But light, even with all its incredible benefits, can cause damaging harm to another when used improperly. Therefore, we must be cautious not to use our God-given light to burn another. Instead, let us be the light at the end of someone else's tunnel. Until we learn to do so, we cannot truly love.

This chapter is dedicated to anyone who has ever found themselves drowning in darkness.

Glasses

Lady in the yellow,
I saw you from a distance.
And I came up to say hello,
I am hoping you will listen.

I know I wasn't in your plans,
I just arose from the masses.
By the way, my name is Lenz,
almost like those in your glasses.

I've known my worth since my birth,
I'm a Father's Day-born gentleman.
I have a way with my words,
I'm the modern-day King Solomon.

But I don't always feel so essential.
I often don't live up to my potential.

I've failed more than I've succeeded.
I've fallen short more than I've exceeded.

I've made choices that I've regretted.
I have a fear of being rejected.

I don't have the greatest appearance.
I may never have a marriage like my parents'.

My life is still searching for guidance.
At night, my mind stays up seeking some silence.

I never ask for assistance,
I tend to hide behind my pride.
I used to deny God's existence,
yet never did he deny mine.

Oh, how special am I?

Still sometimes, I shy
away from attention.
Sometimes, I cry
to take away the tension.

Sometimes, my thoughts
go off on a tangent.
Sometimes, I've fought
an intense intention
to just...

Anyway, back to what I meant to mention.

Lady in the yellow,
I saw you from a distance.
And I came up to say hello,
I was hoping you would listen.

I was standing below and saw you on the rooftop
standing there on the edge.
I, then, felt the distress in your teardrop
kiss the top of my head.

I know you want to jump to your conclusion.
But I promise you, that is not the solution.

Lady in the yellow,
you, too, are someone special.

But we're all fighting a war,
when we're hidden, shattered in the shadows.
There's a lesson in it all,
it's merely a message in a battle.

But despite our cries,
our Christ is
greater than our crisis.

Yes, we are scared.
Yes, we are scarred.
Yet, we are sacred.
Trust me, you are.

So, go ahead and put your hand in mine.
Let us share our hurt and let our scars align.

And if you ever again
find yourself wishing this life ends.

Before that day passes,
just pick up your glasses...
and contact Lenz.

Mask

Every day, he wears a mask.
It's so convincing that no one asks.

They can't see that lies lie in his smile.
Or know he goes home and cries the Nile.
He lives in a lion's den
of lies and denial.

But he never lets his sufferings surface.
So, no one knows he's lost his purpose.

He's tried dealing with his aches
by going to the gym to lift weights,
hoping those weights will lift him up.
But that didn't work out well enough.

He's still seeking something fulfilling.
So, now he eats past the point of a full feeling.
Because his dessert will never desert him,
even while buried under burdens.

Every day, he wears a mask.
And every night, he grabs a flask
then lets whiskey whisk him away.
80-Proof, but no evidence of a better day.

Sometimes, he fights his battles with bottles.
Looking for some light
in each pack of Bud Light.

Sometimes heroin is his hero,
whatever might be right
to save him through the night.

And when, at last,
the evening has passed,
he'll be back to the task
of wearing a mask.

It's so convincing,
they'll never ask.

Man of the Spirit
*A human parallel to the temptation of Christ
as depicted in Matthew 4:1-11 and Luke 4:1-13.*

*I was raised
to always
be a man of the Spirit.
To be a man of God's Word and to fear it.*

*And my parents
made this apparent.*

*In the beginning of my life was the Word.
And the Word was with me.
And the Word became me.
So plainly,*

*I learned
to yearn
to always do what's right.
I tried to fast every day and every night
from every immorality.*

*And I went through the formality
of normality
so that humanity
wouldn't see inside of me
the flesh that was fighting me.*

*Then one day, with my mind in a trance,
the Devil made an entrance.
So intense,
he said:*

39

"Young man of God,
you I applaud.

All your life
you have strived
to be a good and faithful servant.

Through all the rain,
the pain you've gain,
I'm telling you, you don't deserve it.

Still, you've endured
and you've ensured
that you've pleased the Royal One.
But take a look, loyal son.

Look out across to the many nations
and see the men of this generation.

Enjoying their life is their main purpose.
Delighting in everything on this Earth's surface.
The ladies pleasure them at their service
A great man like you deserves this.

All your years you've avoided lust.
But as a man, every day you must

face the temptations
as if you're David Ruffin.
I don't need any translations
to understand this must be rough and

yet, you want to maintain your morals
for many more tomorrows.

But in a sense,
your innocence
is for nothing.
Have you forgotten?

As long as you repent,
the Lord will not relent
to forgive you.
Now I give you
my friendly offer.
Here is Jezebel's daughter.

You don't need to bother
trying to convince
or deceive her.
Just make plans
to receive her.

Cause already,
she is all ready.

I will let her in,
she's a veteran
at giving pleasure and
she'll take you where you've never been.

For too long you've been the better man
This will be cool, ask the weatherman.

So, put your mind at ease
and hear my pleas.
Won't you, please,
let her please?"

To this I replied
with a cry:

"Flee from me, you fallen angel
I won't be falling into
your trickery
to trigger me
into a life of misery.

I refuse to
be reduced to
a life in the absence
of abstinence

So, away from me Satan.
You've been mistaken.
Take the offer
off her.

This ruse
you use
will not prosper."

Then looking astounded,
Lucifer expounded:

"Don't be foolish.
Live life to the fullest.

I know you want to stand on
your standards,
but give that an intermission
and enter this mission.

For, it is written, we've all fallen short
of some sort.
So, stop trying to be the giant.
Stop trying to be defiant.

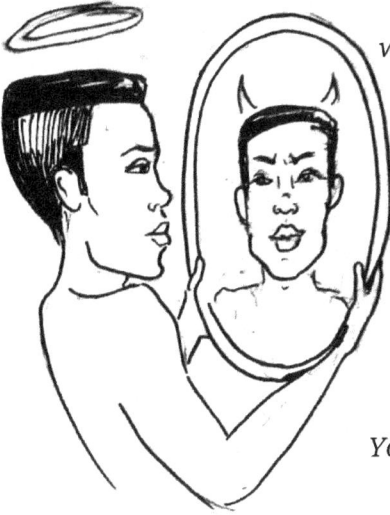

I fathom
we all contain an atom
of Adam
at home.

So, it sounds to me
that resoundingly
we're all bound to be
over the boundaries.

And the fact is
you're attractive.
You will be a magnet to
the magnitude.

So, upon demand,
I, the Demon,
deem
the Redeemer
would change His demeanor
on this misdemeanor.

He'll give you a pass like you're Jerry Rice
for having been so very nice.

43

You've walked that line that's so very thin.
When it comes to heaven,
you're already in.
This is just one of seven
of the deadly sins.
No need to be nervous, see my steady hands?

Have you not once learned
it's not about the wrong turns
you take along the avenue?
It's about what you have in you.
And you have a good heart, haven't you?

You deserve a break.
Now celebrate.
Stop being celibate.
I want your soul, won't you sell a bit?
I won't tell of it.

The God you complain to
will continue to contain you.

Your lust
will be lost
in translation to the Father
Once again I present: Jezebel's daughter.
Take the offer."

Just the same, I exclaimed:

"Away from me Satan.
I am a Saint and
your words may beat on
my eardrums,
but I won't walk to that tempo.
My body is a temple.

Despite your hatred,
I will keep it sacred.
Simple."

Then the Devil declared
with a look of despair:

"I said you were a great man,
I was wrong, certainly.
Her heart's going to break and,
indeed, it is hurting me.

I thought you'd be her surgeon.
But now you're on the verge and
you want to stay a virgin.
Don't you see this is urgent?

I told her
that you were
a good and faithful servant.

I said, to you, there was no equal.
I, the Demon, stated
that you were a lady's hero,
now you don't demonstrate it.

Don't you want to be a hero?
Why don't you demonstrate it?
Be her Superman and demonstrate it!"

So, I threw on a cape
and I penetrated!

I penetrated a bullet
through my innocence.
I penetrated the nails
back in Jesus' hands.

I penetrated the crown of thorns
into His skull.
I penetrated as my morals
penetrated the walls.

I penetrated a sword
right into the Lord.
I penetrated a knife
through my future wife.

I penetrated.
For this sin, I traded
my years of being a role model.
I stepped out of Jesus' shadow
so I could catch a tan
from the rays of the sin.

And I can't say this is planned
by my lack of discipline.
For I've had those lessons
from my adolescence.

Still, I penetrated
and I perpetrated
a crime in God's eyes.
Lord, I apologize.

I pray that my cries
will penetrate Your ears
and you see the fears
running down my cheeks.

Right now, my heart speaks,
and I pray you hear it.
I want to go higher in Your Spirit.

This time I will not trip up
while making my trip up.

There'll be no more hollow hallelujahs.

47

To my future wife,
I apologize
for adding a baggage
to our carriage
of marriage.

I'm sorry I penetrated with no strings attached
and no rings attached.

But from my sin
came my lesson.
I've been transformed
by my transgression.

I have the feature
of a new creature.
I have the anatomy
of another me.

And undoubtedly,
with the God in me
guiding me
I'll be the utmost hero by saving myself.
Saving myself for you.

Until the day you're happily
half of me
because we're joined by "I do."

And then that's when we can join hearts
until the rest of the world has faded.
And although death may do us part,
our love will never, ever be penetrated.

Cracks of your Heart

Take off your joy. Take off your bliss.
Take off your beauty and forget it exists.

Lay that smile of yours down on the floor.
Place your perfection on the knob of the door.

Place your pleasure on my dresser
and undress of any pressure
to conceal the distress that you feel.
Right now, all I want you to wear are your
Achilles' heels.

Because tonight, I want to witness your
weakness,
and sink in your sickness.
I want to seek your secrets
and your forgotten forgiveness.

Let me count the stars in your scars
and learn the languages of your anguishes.
Let me water the flowers in your flaws
to see the blooming of your blemishes.

I want to fly on the wings
of the bird in your burdens.
Show me the stains behind your stage
as I lift up your curtains.

Let me dive deep in your depression,
passed the cheer in your laughter.
I am trying to get down
to the hurt of the matter.

Wrap me in your wrath
as I stroll through your stresses.
I want to partake in your heartache
and read the message in your messes.

Let your pain paint me
as I drown in your frown.
I'll turn your crying to your crown
as your tears tear me down.

Let me wear your wars
and bathe in your battles,
sit in your situations
and swallow your sorrows.

Play me the songs in your wrongs
as I have ten dances with your tendencies.
Let me wander under your wonders
as I faint into your fantasies.

I'll turn your harm into harmony
as I waltz with your faults.
Un-bottle your rebuttals,
as I taste the salts inserted in your insults.

I want to handle every angle of your anger
and wallow in your worry.
I want to follow until I fall in your failures
and soar in your sores and your sorrys.

Remove your rose-colored glasses,
we won't need any lens.
Let me bite into your bitterness
and take a sip of your sins.

I want to regress into your regrets
and get up in your upsets.
I want to have a conversation
with the skeletons in your closet.

Spray me with the mist of your mistakes
and air out the aura of your era of errors.
Let me browse through your bruises
and take a tour of your terrors.

I'll trace a trail of your trials to taste your tests.
Cover up your more as I unlace your less.

Let me open the book of your conscience
so I can dine from your Table of Discontents.

Let me snuggle with your struggles
and cuddle with your troubles.

Unlock the gates of the fences in your defenses,
as I circle your circumstances.
Let me make love with your lows
until we both come to our senses.

I want to have wound up in your wounds
before the sun replaces the moon.

So, consider these words I've spoken
and open your broken.

Let's turn off the lights
and turn on the dark.
Tonight I will find
the cracks of your heart.

IV. *FAITH & FULFILMENT*

God is love. And because you are created in His image and likeness, you too are love.

So, if you are longing for love, look no further than the God within yourself. The truth is, you are more than enough.

If you ever find yourself forgetting that you are worthy of love, just turn to this chapter, light some candles, turn on some music, lay back on your pillow, and let me remind you who you are and whose you are.

"So God created man in his own image,
in the image of God created he him;
male and female created he them." -Genesis 1:27

The Image

Be the image of God in your city.
Fulfill the duty of a Deity.

Do not be too shy to shine.

God should be campaigned
through every campus
until His camp is
composed

of every being
in every building

and He takes a part in
every apartment.

To minister
to the sinister.

To reach the juvenile
who is into denial.

To convert serpents
into servants.

To comfort those who are languished,
those of every language.

53

There are souls
to console
and to counsel
those who've lost control.

To uplift those who have fallen under.
To feed families in famine being hung by hunger.

To fill those who feel a void,
and we cannot avoid
the masses
going through these messes
who just need a message.

So be the image of God in your city.

We need God's intensity
to echo at every level.
To chase away the Devil.
To change the hearts of rebels.

So, we cannot settle
and watch our God, the most Reverent
be faded to irrelevant.

It's demeaning
that some don't know the meaning
of the God we serve
and He deserves

that we ensure His lessons
never lessens.

Let us march forth
and not plead the fifth.

Let us not practice the science of silence.
Let us do our necessary assignments

to change violence
into violins

that simply
play a symphony
of sympathy

amplified
and emphasized
by empathy.

The only strategy
to correct every tragedy
is for us to be the image of God in our city.

*"And as we have borne the image of the earthy,
we shall also bear the image of the heavenly."*
-1 Corinthians 15:49

Blank Canvas

Lord, make me an image of You!

*At times, this life seems senseless.
But, as long as I'm in this,
I'll be a blank canvas.*

*I want to feel the faint touch
of Your sacred paintbrush.*

*Give me all of Your traits.
Make me Your self-portrait.*

*Make me an image of You,
I'm in need of Your anointing.
Pour oil on my head
to make me Your oil painting.*

*How great Thou art.
Make me Your work of art.*

*Brush me boldly.
Color me holy, wholly.*

*And when the wind of this lonely
world blows coldly,*

*cover me with two coats of paint.
Paint me into a saint.*

Give me fades of faith
and a trace of grace.

Give me a dash of Your diligence.
An ink of Your intelligence.

A tint of Your tenderness.
A rub Your righteousness.

Polish me in Your purity.
Scrape off my insecurity.

Give me a kiss of Your kindness.
Give me a dye of divineness.

Make me die so that Your beauty
may be lived through me.

Even when the pain rains on,
do not let my colors run.

And if I try to run away from Your eyes,
Lord, color me inside of the lines.

And give me highlights of humility.
So I can dig past my dignity

to let your face be seen in me
in every vicinity.

And though the world may pity me
I want to be the epitome

Of a man who's achieved victory
Over all iniquity

Because my metaphors and similes
Cannot afford infinity

My wordplays and rhymes
cannot purchase me time,

but I can use them to shine
Your face through my lines.

Make me an image of you!

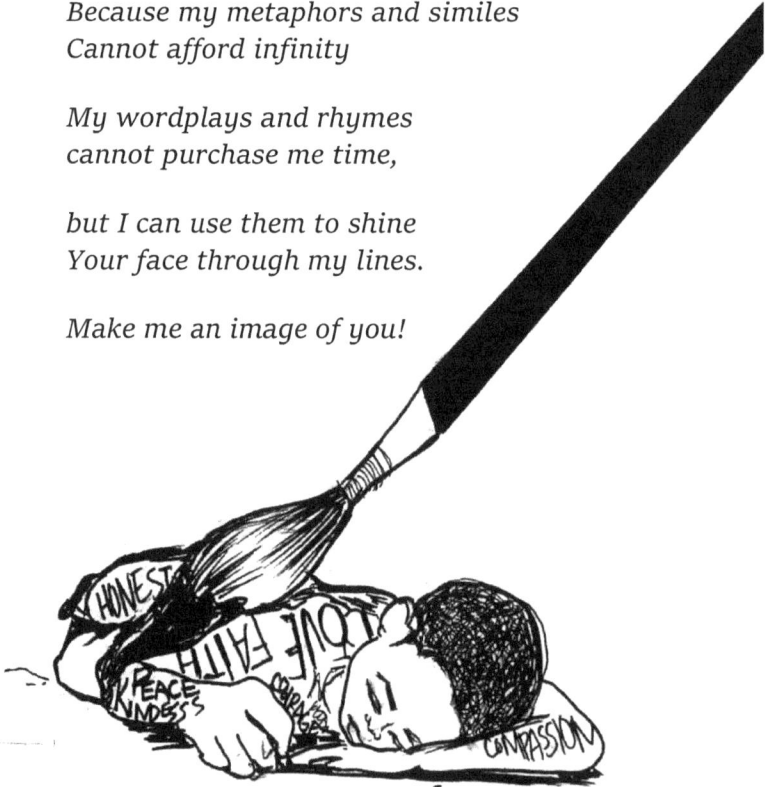

More than merely your caricature.
Fill me with your caring nature.
Make me resemble your reflection in the mirror.

As the end of time draws nearer,
draw me into a picture
of perfection.

Give me the complexion
of a Christian.

It's my mission
not to run with the herd,
but to walk with the Word.

Be my instructor
And structure
me into a sculpture
of the Scripture.

Give me textures
of Your lectures.

I want to be molded
into a model
of the Gospel.

So that I know
wherever I go,

for as long as I'm living,
in whatever setting I'm sitting
I'll be a spitting
...image of You!

Shape me into Your servant.
Keep me firm in
Your sermons.

I want to soak in Your teachings like a sponge
then use them to wipe away all my wrongs.

Give me a zeal
the world can't steal.

Let my status
be a statue
of Your statutes.

Chisel in me charity.
Give me cuts of clarity.

Give me patterns of Your patience
and outlines of obedience.

Give me replicas of Your reverence.
Give me love for my brethren.

Give me forms of forgiveness.
Wash away every weakness.

Give me copies of Your compassion.
So all of my interactions
and every fraction
of my actions
may be loyal and true.

Dear Lord, make me an image of You!

Phenomenal Man

*(An homage to the immortal Maya Angelou.
Inspired by her classic "Phenomenal Woman")*

*Some gentlemen wonder where my secret lies.
I'm not strong, nor built along
a bodybuilder's size.
But when I start to tell them,
they think I'm telling lies.*

*I say, it's in the flirt of my charm.
The flash of my grin.
The warmth in my arm.
The cleft of my chin.*

*I am a man phenomenally.
Phenomenal man, that's me.*

*I walk into a room just as cool as you please.
As I come in, the ladies stand
and they greet me with ease.
Then they swarm around me,
a hive of honey bees.*

*I say, it's in the class of clothes
and the firm of my stand.
The suave of my pose
and the touch of my hand.*

*I am a man phenomenally.
Phenomenal man, that's me.*

Gals themselves have wondered
what they see in me.
They try so much,
but they can't touch
my inner mystery.
When I try to show them,
they say they still can't see.

I say, it's in the line of my walk.
The love of my help.
The wit in my talk.
The being of myself.

I am a man phenomenally
Phenomenal man, that's me.

Now you understand just why
my head's not bowed.
I don't shout, Or jump about
or have to talk real loud.
When you see me passing,
it ought to make you proud.

I say, it's in the range of my mind.
The will in my eyes.
The gift of rhymes.
The God in my life.

I am a man phenomenally.
Phenomenal man, that's me.

Royalty

Let me speak of the greatness that is You.
Let me turn up the volume
on your value.

Let me raise
your praise
and promote
your prominence.

Let me magnify
your magnificence.

Let me reveal
your reverence
and relay
your relevance.

Let me elevate
the elements
of your elegance
with eloquence.

Let me offer your intelligence
enough evidence
to believe
when you breathe,
you exhale excellence.

To know, without hesitance,
you are more prestigious
than presidents.
You set the precedence.

63

You are royalty!
And no one can emulate
your eminence.

This is real.
You are regal.
You are royal.

I say this without any bias,
for you are children of the Highest.
Ah, yes!

You are akin
to a King
who is one of a kind.
You are transformed
by the renewing of your mind.

There is a deity in your identity.

God dwells within your atmosphere.
So, don't be afraid of the things that most fear.

The God in you is Sovereign.
It surpasses Superman
in every content.
You can do things that even Clark can't.

Although it's beautiful
to model modesty,
it would be a travesty
to not know
you are more than magical,
you are majesty.
You are part of a dynamic dynasty,
honestly.

So never hang your head down
and cause your crown to fall.
When others fall short, you must stand tall.

For you are an emperor or an empress.
Even when you feel like you do not impress,
know you're more than a prince or princess.
You are priceless.

Your status
is god and goddess.
Ah, yes!

You are not just any species,
you are special.

You are phenomenal.
Never inferior.
You're even fairer.
Like a Pharaoh,
you are a ruler,
but of perfect measure.

Whatever may transpire,
let God guard and guide your entire empire.

In your royalty,
never depart from loyalty.

Never allow anarchy
into your monarchy.

Let wisdom
build your kingdom.

Watch what is thrown
at your throne.
Although none are without sin,
they'll still cast the first stone.

As you reign,
some will try to rain
on your parade.
Beware of wolves clothed in sheep masquerade.

Ladies and gentlemen,
you're not general.
Your genius is genuine.

Your worth is birthed from within,
so your importance
is never imported.

Be attentive
of your attitude.
Know that the magnitude
of your magnificence
is magnetic.
You are always attractive.

66

If by happenstance
you find your happiness
being hindered,
remember your standard.

You are a royal priesthood,
a peculiar people.
Whatever issues
life has issued,
you will be greater than, never equal.

It is a privilege
to stand upon the ledge
of your knowledge.

So, Kings and Queens.
Superior beings.

As you walk about,
don't lose your crown
in the crowd.

Do not let your heart be hardened.
Let the fruits of the spirit grace your garden.
And never let your royalty be forgotten.

Pair of Hands

Ladies and gentlemen,
I need a pair of hands.
I have been shot by
the arrow of arrogance.

Ever since,
my common sense
has me convinced

that I was born so
normal,
then blossomed
to awesome.
So therein lies the problem.

My understanding
tells me I am standing
at outstanding.

So, when I sit,
you better believe it,
I am seated
conceited.

I've taken a tumble
and stumbled
from humble.

But honestly,
how could I live modestly
when I do everything so flawlessly?

68

"Everything" is what I do best.
I am the key to success.

I can do things that no one can understand.
I can take the bounce out of winter,
so that it doesn't spring.

I can catch summer so that it doesn't fall.
Yes, I mean it. I can do it all.

I've tried
to hide
my pride,

but it seems
my self-esteem

still soars higher than an eagle.
And my ego
won't let me go.

So once again,
I say this, my friends,
I need a pair of hands...

TO CLAP FOR ME!!

Yes, clap for me!
Because I'm the only business, like a monopoly.
I am a prodigy.
So, my ego will make no apology.

In fact, I should be wrapped
and carry a bow since I'm so gifted.
I even speak to myself just to feel uplifted.

No meterstick
can measure my leadership.

In the class of grand men, I'm valedictorian.
I will go down in the books, tell your historian.

So, applause
for the cause.

Give me all the fanfare
I can bare.

Or it'll keep
my sleep.

It'll kidnap
my nap.

It'll arrest
my rest.

So, release
my peace
by showing me I'm the best.

Put me on Cloud Nine
to cloud my
proud mind.

Fill my head like a piñata.
Make it frank a la Sinatra.

Clap. Oh, bravo!
I know I'm so...
um, indescribable.
Is my head about to explode?
It is probable.

But it's unstoppable,
so I won't be ending it.
Even if I don't say I'm the best, I'll be thinking it.

Will I ever cause
the applause
to pause?

Nah, that's not even plausible.
Where would the applauses go?

I'm so sorry,
but I need all the glow and the glory.

I need it on every occasion,
in every location,
from every position.

So, please give me my consolation
Go on and give me my standing ovation!!

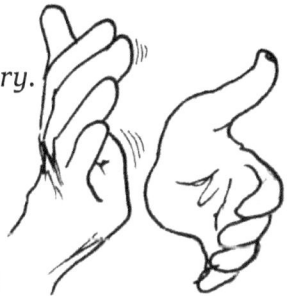

71

V. *FLIRTATIONS & FOREVER*

Following all of the frowns, the false-flags, and the failures, you have found your forever. And isn't it beautiful when the affection is mutual?

You know that feeling you feel for your forever? Those emotions so remarkable that you can't even put them into words? Worry not! I've found the words for you. Well, almost.

Anyway, read this chapter to your lover. Your best friend. Your partner. Your forever. And then read it to them again. In fact, don't ever stop reading it to them.

Addiction

You are my favorite prescription.
You are the prescription
that fits no description.

You are more marvelous
than the medicine of a pharmacist.

You are the pill
that can peel
away the pain
of my sickness.

You are the drug
that can drag
away the strain
of my weakness.

Whatever the diagnosis,
I have noticed
that for your mastery,
no misery
is a mystery.

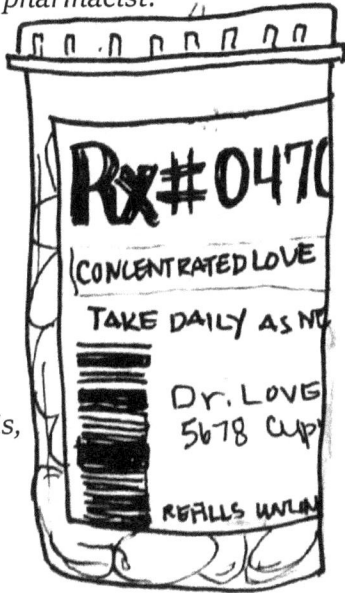

Because a couple cups of your care
can cure the core
of any hurt or disease.

A bit of a bottle of your beauty
can get to the bottom of any bother,
and can do so with ease.

73

A spoonful of your spirit
can alleviate all ailments
when I'm affected by afflictions.

For that reason,
you have risen
to be an addition
to my addictions.

And my craving never lessens.
I yearn for each pint of your presence.

To be captured
by a capsule
of your humor can heal
a whole room.

And a grain
of your grace
can erase
an old wound.

So, I wish upon a scar,
that for my eternity,
I'll always find tranquility
in each sip of your serenity.

April Showers

They say April showers
bring May flowers.
Yet, I was always a skeptic.
Never did I accept it.

Because my calendar was always
filled with April days
that I spent beside my garden
in the painful rain.

Calling out to the sun:
"Won't you please save me from
the hurt of this storm?"

Screaming out "Mayday!"
and praying for a May day
that may never come.

I waited and wished
for a flower to appear,
but all I had received
was raindrops on my tears.

Then one fine day,
there came blue skies
and a rose arose
before my eyes.

Flourished by the rain
of her hair down to her shoulders.
Nourished by the rays
of her smile, which no man can look over.

Mother nature
can't compare to her human nature.

She's a rose blooming with grace
and every petal of her face
is far beyond perfect.

I know I've been warned
that every rose has its thorn,
but the pain would be worth it.

I didn't need to take in
any of the May mayhem
and never spent an hour
sailing on the Mayflower.

Still, I discovered this rose.
And I know the saying goes
that when life's stress exposes
to stop and smell the roses.

Still, I never will have forgotten
Her, the prettiest rose in any garden.

Reds and Whites

Damsel in distress, it is so clear
that these past 12 months was not your year.
I can see your pain. I can hear your fears.
Global warming can't dry your shedding tears.

But your courage deserves an applause.
Witnessing it makes me better than I was.
To thank you on Christmas, I'll make it my cause
to ease all you hurt by being your Santa Claus.

I'm making my list and checking it twice.
It tells me you have been naughtily nice.
Here I'm dressed in these reds and these whites.
All I want is the rights
to be your Santa Claus.

I'll to travel you back to your childhood.
When Christmas placed you in a wild mood,
and the sun couldn't shine like your smile would.
Oh, for a while could
I just be your Santa Claus?

I'm aware your year's been a violent fight,
but put on that smile that is vibrant white
and get ready for a not-so-silent night.
There's no wrong that I can't right
if I am your Santa Claus.

I don't care for carolers,
your voice is all I want to hear.
From your whispers to your laughter,
it's all music to my ears.
Forget the milk and cookies,
please just feed me with your cheers.
For as long as I am here,
I will be your Santa Claus.

I'll dim the Christmas lights to see your glow
Bright enough to melt North Pole's winter snow.
Rudolph's nose can't equal the shine you'll show.
'Tis the season I'll make it so
when I am your Santa Claus.

The ceiling will be our mistletoe.
The lights and music will be so low.
But you won't have to be solo.
So let the whistle blow
to start my reign as your Santa Claus.

Know well that Noel can make it all well.
Let Kris Kringle come and jingle your bells.
Step out of the despair where you dwell.
Secret Santa won't tell
that I am your Santa Claus.

I'll make it my business
to fulfill your wish list.
But all that you need is this.
Let these stockings witness
the power of your own Santa Claus

So, this December 25th,
let me make truth of a myth.
It will be the greatest gift
when you see that you are with
your one and only Santa Claus.

Chemical Excellence

Sugar, spice and everything nice.
These were the ingredients chosen
to create the perfect little girl.
But God added an extra ingredient
to the concoction:

Chemical Excellence!

It's true.
In you,
God added Chemical Excellence.

But even with those elements
God, in all His eminence
still had more work to do.

Because "Everything Nice"
would only suffice
in creating a slice
of a lady like you.

So, God the Chef, stirred you
in a bowl of virtue
for your price to be
far above rubies.

And then you were tossed in
a pot of attraction
so your looks could be
far above beauty.

Beauty, both physical and spiritual.
Lyrical and biblical.

Lady of Proverbs 31,
that makes you numerical.
And at last, God's work was done,
He cooked up a new miracle.

So, all angry ingredients can Rest-In-Peace.
For you are the greatest of God's recipes.

Cupid's Needle

To you, nurse of mine
Here's a nursery rhyme:

Nurse of mine, would you mind
being my nurse for all time?

And you won't even need those needles
or the inches of these syringes.

For I am shot by Cupid's Needle.

Your smile pierces through my vein
And your words pierce through my brain.

Your beauty injects my eyes
and when I think I've had enough,
your virtue injects my heart
and I find myself bleeding love.

I am, indeed, bleeding love
but please just let me.
For you, I'll bleed a flood of blood
until I'm drowning in that red sea.

Then I'll part it like Moses
and escape from death's snare.
Still, I know it'd be worth it
to be nursed by your care.

Paradise

My dear tree planted by the rivers of water:

I pray that you savor
the fruits of your labor.
May you find favor
to bear fruits of each flavor.

May God keep it as so.
May you reap what you sow.

May everything you've planted
be painted

into a paradise
to every pair of eyes.

May God be the guardian
who guards your garden.

May God always intercede
to blossom your inner seed

so you may grow a tree
of poetry

with leaves
that never leave.

For you deserve every inch
of every branch.

__Heavy Breathing__

What is the true meaning of love?
Is it a feeling from above?

Is it proven
with diamond earrings,
heart beating,
and heavy breathing?

Does it require the words,
or is it said with words unheard?

Does it need the approval of man,
or just that of the voice within?

Is it something that must be earned?
Is it still love if unreturned?

Does love allow one the option
of abstinence from interaction?

Is it love, is it true
until the day you say I do?

Well, there's no need to all this ponder,
love may always be a wonder.

I may not know what true love means
But I can say from what I've seen

So, what does true love mean to me?
It's the lady in the mirror whom you see.

Butterflies

A night of passion
between mutual attractions
changed her life in ways she couldn't imagine.

A moment of pleasure
shook and shocked her beyond measure
and blessed her
with unexpected treasure.

Suddenly there was more
than just butterflies in her stomach.

Feeling unprepared, fear fills her mind.
She tells her parents through tear-filled eyes.

And they tell her she can't stay
unless there's a wedding by Wednesday.

But the future father
remains farther.

Her friends line up in a row
to tell her to follow Roe.

But her mind is made.
She is swayed by Wade.

She continues to carry life in her womb,
and tries to carry love in her heart.
But the world wants to tear her apart.

She is judged as a sinner
by every eye that has seen her.
Full belly and empty finger.

She hears society's mutter
of how she is fit to be an unfit mother.

She searches for her smile,
but the world won't let her.
They want the name of her child
spelled with a scarlet letter.

But many months later,
she works through the labor.

And then behold,
she holds
the daughter
the world tried to doubt her.

She stares in her baby's eyes
and found love like no other.

She realizes at the heart of the matter
the sorrows and the sorrys she suffered,
can't compare to the joys of being a mother.

Simile for her Smile

Here at the altar he stands,
soon to be altered into a new man.

He patiently waits for his rib to join his side.
And, behold, at long last, here comes the bride.

His eyes are struck by the essence
of her presence.
And suddenly time has frozen the seconds.

As he looks her way, she walks up his stares.
And there...
There is the answer to all of his prayers.

This dazzling damsel in this dress
coming to save him from distress.

My God, she is gorgeous!
Words haven't been invented
that are intended
to do her justice.

For her beauty
cannot be bottled
into consonants and vowels.

There's not a word
worthy to be her award.

No metaphor
he might afford
may form
a phrase to praise her ways.

There is no grammar
to glorify her glowing glamor.

No adjective adjusted
comes adjacent
to her style.

Seemingly,
there is no simile
for her smile.

The volume
of her value
speaks louder than words can tell us.

The radius
of her radiance
makes the sunlight jealous.

The elements
of her elegance
speak secrets of the Angel's features.

In her creation,
God went beyond
the standard procedures.

He is awed.
Is it odd
that looking at her, he sees God?

She is goddess.
She is flawless.

From his perception,
she is perfection.

Here at the altar he stands,
being grazed by her grace.
He's finding salvation at the sight of her face.

He's swimming in the depth of her eyes.
And if she should wave,
he would drown in her tides.
His tongue is tied.

But the magic
of her majesty,
he cannot repel.
L-O-V-E,
he fell under her spell.

He is mesmerized.
But no expression he has memorized
can be inserted in a sentence
to suitably state this instance.

She is more than pronouns
can pronounce.

He understands that
stanzas
cannot stand to
speak sufficiently of the modesty
in her majesty.

Nor of the humility
in her humanity.

She is an anomaly.
She ascends above all alliterations
and any acknowledgements
of an analogy.
She is beyond all terminology.

Nevertheless, for the rest of his life,
he will search for nouns and verbs.
Even if he never finds
her the words she deserves.

She will still be the woman whom he worships.
And she is surely worth it.

So, here at the altar he meets her face to face
as their souls meet faith to faith.

And one thing he knows for certain,
this is his moment of fate.

Patience
was a heavy
burden...

but she was surely
worth the weight.

I cannot write you a poem.

My dearest Love,

I'm writing you this letter
to issue my apology.
For I had a plan so clever,
in wish you'd be proud of me.

I was going to write you a poem.
All by my lonesome.

A poem to make you blush
into a mild tan.
To even make your tears cry
and your smile grin.

But at last, alas, woe is me.
I cannot write you this poetry.

For it would not do you justice.
Gorgeous,
you must trust this.

I cannot write you a poem,
I hope this doesn't hurt you.
But words cannot fathom
how to verbalize your virtue.

For even if I gathered words
as numerous as the stars.
I could never write a poem
better than the poem you are.

THANK YOU SO MUCH FOR READING!!! :~)

*Tell all your friends about this book
and please send letters of encouragement to:*

Email: LenzDalusmaPoetry@gmail.com
Facebook.com/RhymeAndShine
Address: PO Box 598, Immokalee, FL 34143

*Be sure to be on the lookout
for future books by Lenz Dalusma.*

Inspired by this book?

*Use the following blank page
to write a poem of your own. ;)*

Title:

Author:

ABOUT THE AUTHOR:

Hailing from Haiti, Lenz Dalusma is a renowned poet and spoken word artist who has garnered much praise and accolades over the years for his creative writing style and captivating spoken word performances.

Lenz is also the founder of *Rhyme&Shine Poetry Ministry*, an organization of poets dedicated to sharing their spoken art in various venues and to the benefit of countless causes.

Contact info:
RhymeAndShine.org
YouTube.com/LenzDalusma
Facebook.com/RhymeAndShineMinistry
Email: RhymeAndShine@gmail.com